Contents

About the Book

"Nothing succeeds like success."
—Alexandre Dumas the Elder, 1854

And no other math resource helps kids succeed like Scholastic Great Math Practice! For classroom or at-home use, this exciting series for kids in grades 1 through 5 provides invaluable reinforcement and practice for math skills such as:

- ❑ number sense and concepts
- ❑ patterns, reasoning and logic
- ❑ basic operations and computations
- ❑ words problems
- ❑ time, money, and measurement
- ❑ fractions and decimals
- ❑ geometry and basic shapes
- ❑ graphs, charts, tables ... and more!

Each book contains loads of challenging puzzles, inviting games, and clever practice pages to keep kids delighted and excited as they strengthen their basic math skills.

What makes *Scholastic Great Math Practice* so solid?

- The chapters are aligned to the scope and progression of the NCERT syllabus. This ensures students are engaging with the worksheets in parallel to classroom lessons.
- Each practice page in the series reinforces a specific, age-appropriate skill as outlined by the NCERT.
- These skills give students the ability to interact with the mathematics they see and experience around them, fully meeting the objectives of the NCF.

Take the lead and help kids succeed with *Scholastic Great Math Practice*.
Parents and teachers agree: No one helps kids succeed like Scholastic!

SCHOLASTIC

GRADE 2

Great Math Practice

Previously published as Scholastic Success with Maths by Scholastic

Published by Scholastic India Pvt. Ltd.

A subsidiary of Scholastic Inc., New York, 10012 (USA).

Publishers since 1920, with international operations in Canada, Australia, New Zealand, the United Kingdom, India and Hong Kong.

For information regarding permission, write to:
Scholastic India Pvt. Ltd.
A-27, Ground Floor, Bharti Sigma Centre
Infocity - 1, Sector 34, Gurgaon (Haryana) 122001
Email: education@scholastic.co.in

First edition: 2017
Reprinted: July 2025

ISBN-13: 978-93-5275-288-1

Printed at Shiv Shakti Printing and trading Co., Haryana

Shapes, Sides, and Corners

Name ______________________________ Date ______________

Complete the sentences about shapes.

1.

This is a ____________________.

This shape has ________ sides.

This shape has ________ corners.

2.

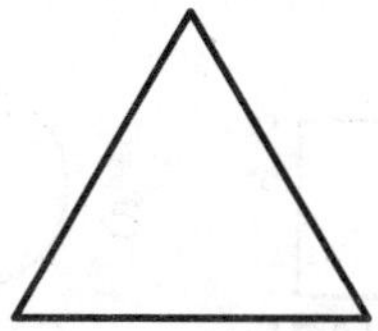

This is a ____________________.

This shape has ________ sides.

This shape has ________ corners.

3.

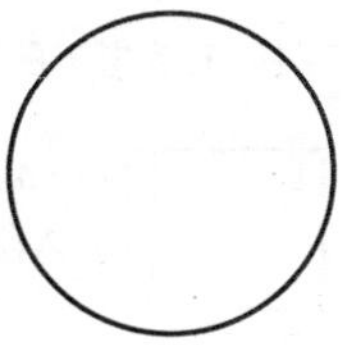

This is a ____________________.

This shape has ________ sides.

This shape has ________ corners.

4.

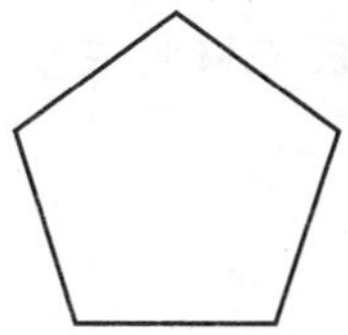

This is a ____________________.

This shape has ________ sides.

This shape has ________ corners.

5. Draw a square. Then, draw a line through it to divide it in half to make two rectangles.

6. Draw a square.Then, draw a line through it to divide it in half to make two triangles.

Shape Gaper

Name ______________________________ Date ______________

FLAT SHAPES HAVE LENGTH AND WIDTH.

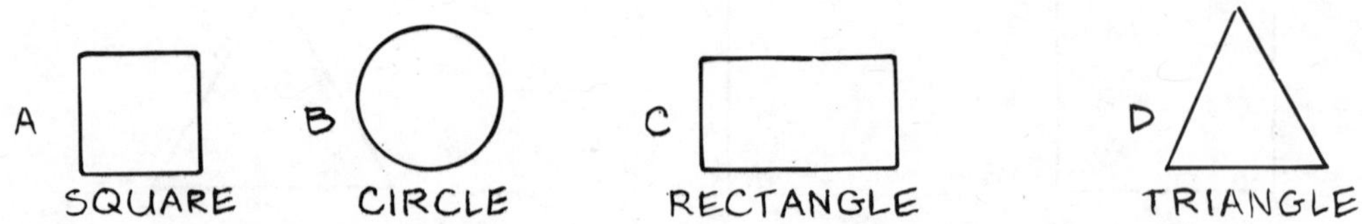

SOLID SHAPES HAVE LENGTH AND WIDTH AND DEPTH.

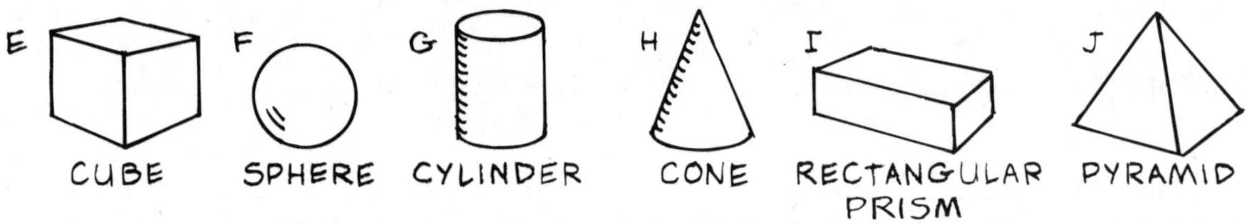

MATCH THE SHAPES WITH THESE OBJECTS. USE THE LETTERS ABOVE.

A.		B.		C.	
1.	BALL	1.	COMPACT DISC	1.	ROAD MARKER
2.	WASTEBASKET	2.	AN ORANGE	2.	FLAG
3.	RING	3.	A FLAG	3.	SHEET OF PAPER
4.	POSTAGE STAMP	4.	A BUILDING	4.	FLASHLIGHT
5.	BIRDHOUSE	5.	FISH BOWL	5.	SOUP CAN
6.	CRAYON BOX	6.	CHILD'S BLOCK	6.	POSTER
7.	ICE CUBE	7.	CHECKERS (GAME)	7.	BASEBALL
8.	APOLLO SPACECRAFT	8.	A SAIL ON A SMALL BOAT	8.	TRAIN CAR
9.	TRASH BARREL	9.	CEREAL BOX	9.	A DIME
10.	JAR	10.	PLANET EARTH	10.	PHOTOGRAPH
11.	ENVELOPE	11	STICK OF BUTTER	11.	WORLD GLOBE

Roll, Slide, Spin?

Name ____________________________________ Date ______________

Decide if these objects roll, slide or spin. Put a tick in the box. Remember, they may do more than one of these.

	Roll	Slide	Spin
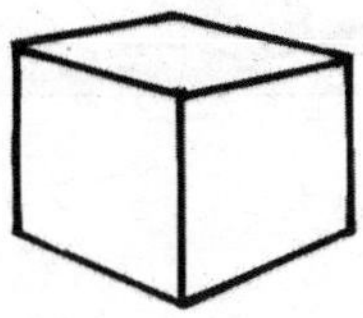			

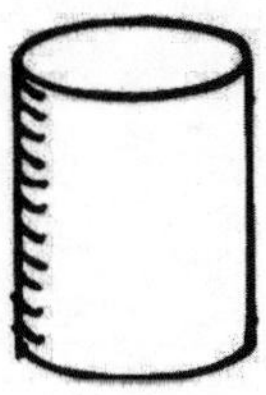			

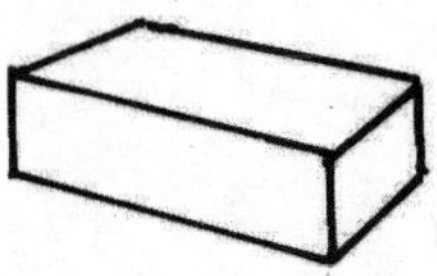			
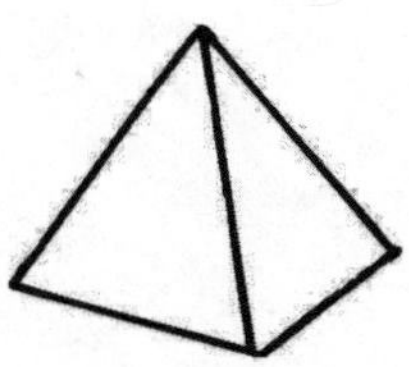			

Tall Tower

Name ______________________ Date ____________

Make a tower, as tall as you can, using these shapes:

Three 

Two 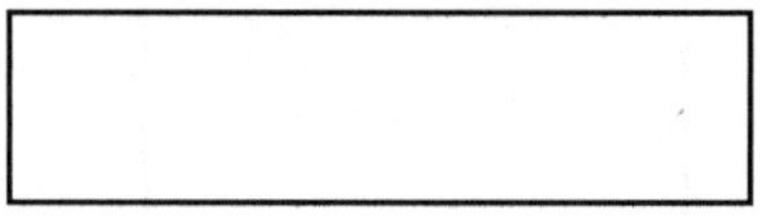

Two 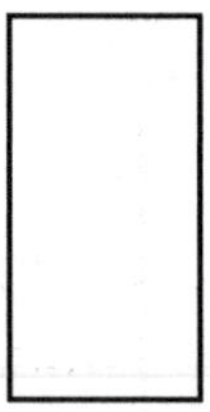

One 

Order Recorder

Name ______________________ Date ____________

WRITE THE MISSING NUMBERS.

1. 164, 165, 166, ____
2. 33, ____ , ____
3. 41, ____ , ____, 44
4. 15, ____, 17, ____, 19
5. ____, ____, ____, 76
6. 29, 30, ____, ____, 33

WRITE WHAT COMES NEXT.

7. 2 4 6 8 ____ ____ ____ ____
8. 3 6 9 12 ____ ____ ____ ____

WRITE THE NUMBERS BETWEEN 82 AND 89.

9. 82 ____, ____, ____, ____, ____, ____, 89

WRITE before OR after.

10. ROOM 479 COMES ________ ROOM 478.
11. PAGE 53 COMES ________ PAGE 63.
12. 15th STREET COMES ________ 12th STREET.
13. ROW 7 COMES ________ ROW 12.
14. JUNE 29 COMES ________ JUNE 30.
15. EXIT 15 COMES ________ EXIT 22.

How Many?

Name ____________________________ Date ______________

Which is the correct sentence? Tick it.

1. 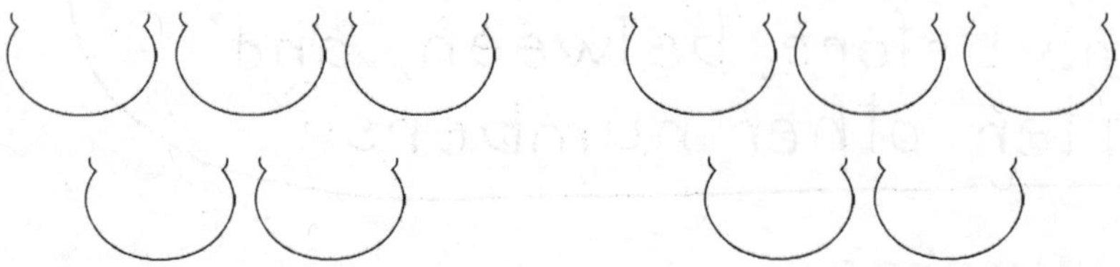

5 + 5

2 + 5

2. 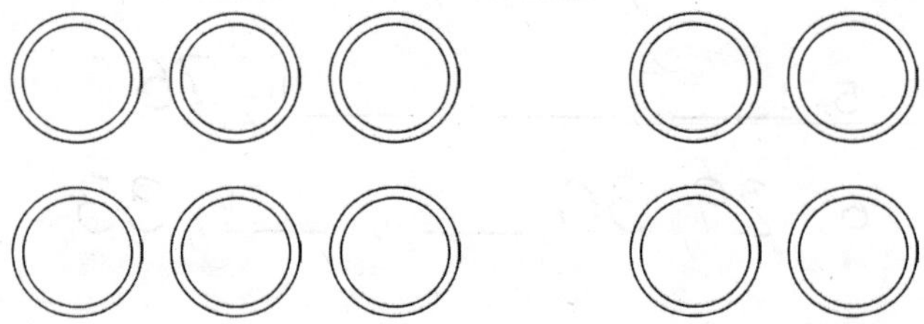

6 + 6

6 + 4

3. 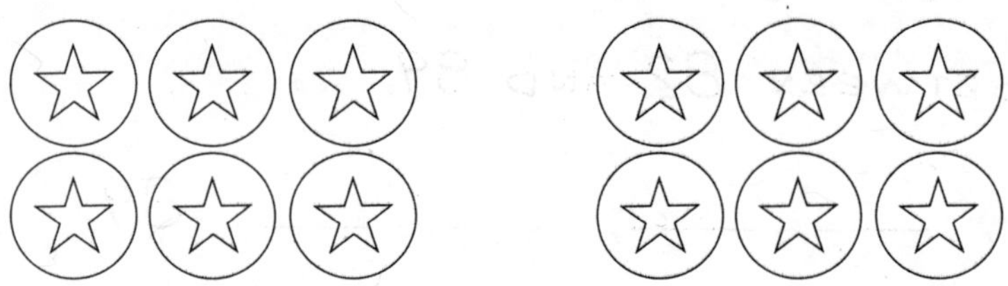

6 + 6

2 + 6

4. 

2 + 5

2 + 3 + 4

5. 

3 + 3

3 + 3 + 3

How Many Legs?

Name ______________________ Date ____________

Fill in the blanks.

1. How many legs on

1 turkey ______	3 turkeys ______
2 turkeys ______	4 turkeys ______

2. How many legs on

1 cat ______	3 cats ______
2 cats ______	4 cats ______

3. How many legs on

1 ladybird ______	3 ladybirds ______
2 ladybirds ______	4 ladybirds ______

4. How many legs on

1 spider ______	3 spiders ______
2 spiders ______	4 spiders ______

5. How many legs on

1 squid ______	6 squid ______
2 squid ______	7 squid ______
3 squid ______	8 squid ______
4 squid ______	9 squid ______
5 squid ______	10 squid ______

Groups & Sets

Name ______________________ Date ____________

1. 

There are ____________ groups of stars.
There are ____________ stars in each group.

2. 

There are ____________ groups of apples.
There are ____________ apples in each group.

3. 

There are ____________ shelves of cups.
There are ____________ cups in each shelf.

4. 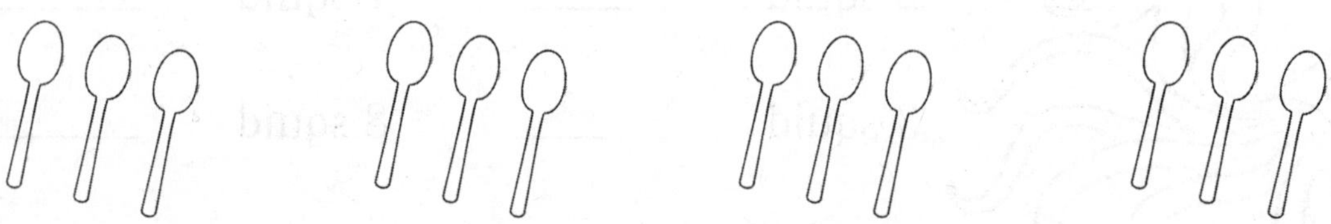

There are ____________ sets of spoons.
There are ____________ spoons in each set.

Zoo Weigh-In

Name ______________________________ Date ______________

Jiven's class went to the zoo. The children tried to guess which baby animal was the heaviest. Look at the animals below. Arrange them in weight order—from lightest to heaviest. Can you draw an animal that looks heavier than the seal but lighter than the deer?

Heavy or Light?

Name ______________________________ Date ______________

1. Which is heaviest? Circle it.

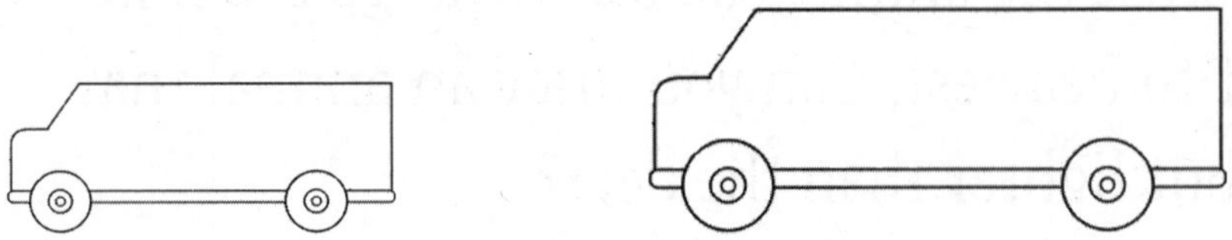

A. B. C.

2. Which is lightest? Circle it.

A. B. C.

3. Which is heaviest? Circle it.

A. B. C.

4. Which is lightest? Circle it.

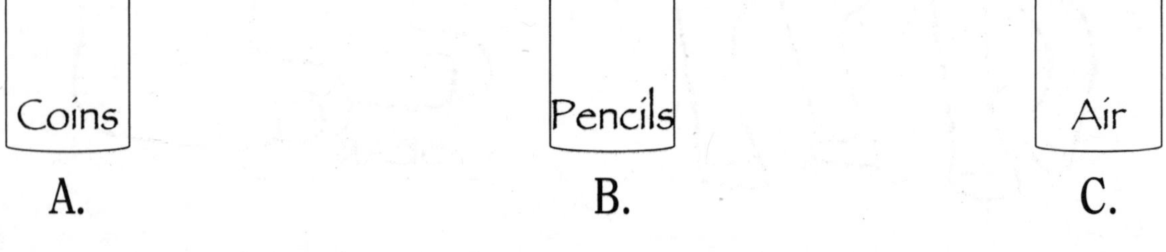

A. B. C.

Un-Balanced

Name ______________________________ Date ______________

Place the items on the beam balance by drawing lines.

1. 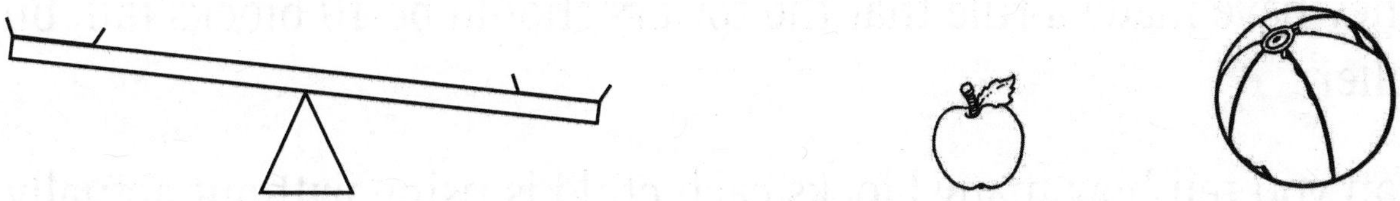

2. 

3. 

4. 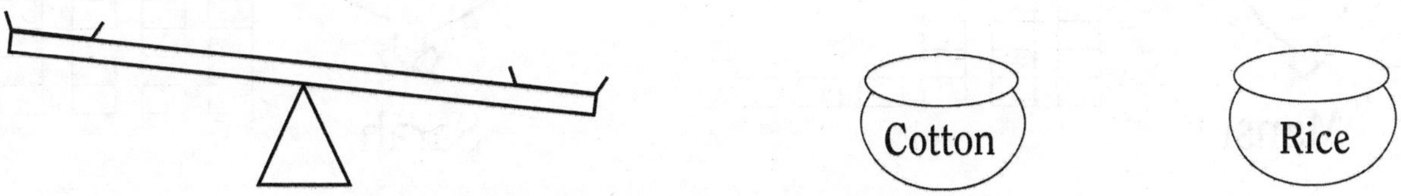

5. 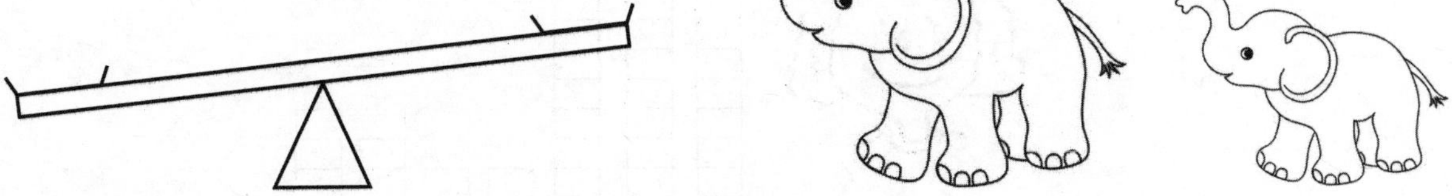

Tall Tens-Towers

Name ______________________ Date ____________

Rishabh and his friends are making towers out of building blocks.

They have made a rule that the towers should be 10 blocks tall, but not taller.

Can you tell how many blocks each child is using without actually counting them?

Rishabh

Lalit

Mansi

Sarah

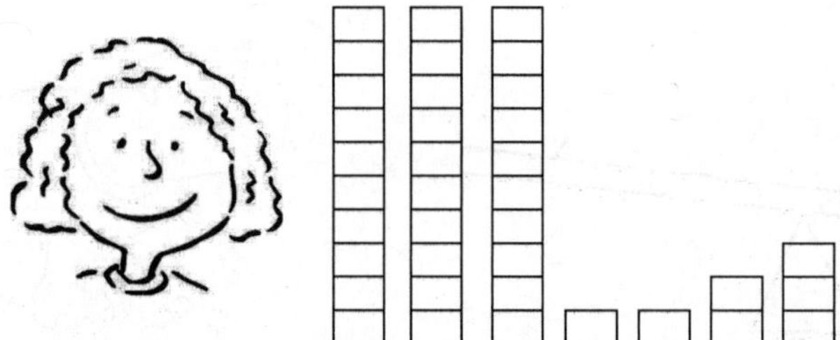

Mini

Tennis Tens

Name ______________________________ Date ______________

Mayank and his friends are collecting tennis balls from the courts in the tennis stadium. He knows that one bucket can hold 10 tennis balls. How many balls have Mayank and his friends collected?

One bucket contains 10 tennis balls.

1. 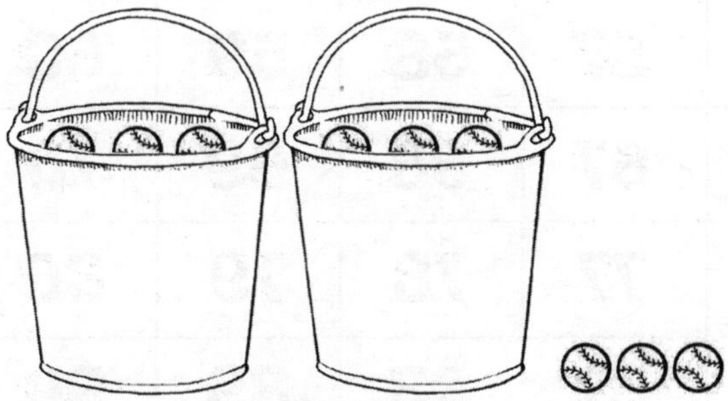

Practice Court A

2. 

Clay Court

3. 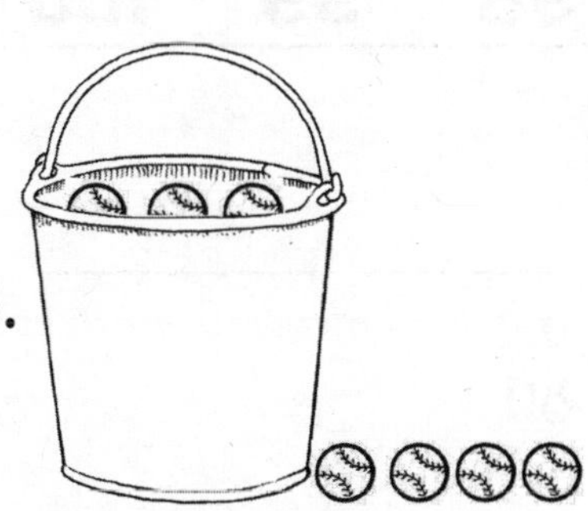

Grass Court

4. 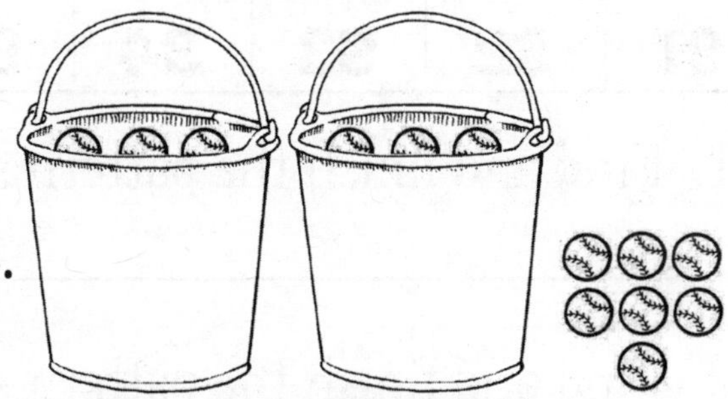

Clay Court Grand

5. 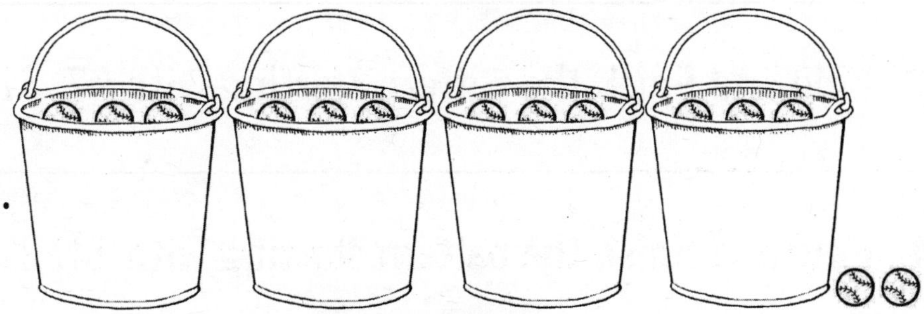

Queen Court

Picking Out Patterns

Name ______________________ Date ____________

On the 100th day of school, everyone in Pat's class picked out patterns on the 100 Chart. Look at the chart below.

1	2	3	4	5	6	7	8	9	10
11	12	13	14	15	16	17	18	19	20
21	22	23	24	25	26	27	28	29	30
31	32	33	34	35	36	37	38	39	40
41	42	43	44	45	46	47	48	49	50
51	52	53	54	55	56	57	58	59	60
61	62	63	64	65	66	67	68	69	70
71	72	73	74	75	76	77	78	79	80
81	82	83	84	85	86	87	88	89	90
91	92	93	94	95	96	97	98	99	100

1. Find and finish the pattern starting with 2, 12, 22

____

2. Find and finish the pattern starting with 100, 90, 80

____

3. Find and finish the pattern starting with 97, 87, 77

____

4. Find and finish the pattern starting with 11, 22, 33

____

AB Pattern

Name ______________________________ Date ______________

A B A B A B

A pattern can have two things repeating. This is called an "AB" pattern.

1. Look around the room. What "AB" patterns do you see?
   Draw one "AB" pattern in the box.

2. Use red and blue crayons to colour the numbers in the chart using an "AB" pattern.

Hundred's Chart

1	2	3	4	5	6	7	8	9	10
11	12	13	14	15	16	17	18	19	20
21	22	23	24	25	26	27	28	29	30
31	32	33	34	35	36	37	38	39	40
41	42	43	44	45	46	47	48	49	50
51	52	53	54	55	56	57	58	59	60
61	62	63	64	65	66	67	68	69	70
71	72	73	74	75	76	77	78	79	80
81	82	83	84	85	86	87	88	89	90
91	92	93	94	95	96	97	98	99	100

Use this rule:

1 = red
2 = blue
3 = red
4 = blue, and so on

The blue numbers are **even numbers.** They can be split evenly into 2 whole numbers.

The red numbers are **odd numbers.** They cannot be split evenly into 2 whole numbers.

Car Confusion

Name ______________________________ Date ______________

Cross out the number that breaks the pattern. Write the correct number below it.

Line up!

Name ______________________________ Date ______________

Look at the pattern in the first two rows. Then, use the same rule to complete the pattern in the third row.

A.

4	8	12
1	5	9
7		

B.

6	9	12
8	11	14
5		

C.

2	10	18
4	12	20
	18	26

D.

5	10	15
35	40	45
	25	

E.

7	14	21
1	8	15
		29

F.

2	11	20
7	16	25
9		

Pansy's Picture Patterns

Name ______________________________ Date ____________

Pansy has lots of hobbies. Her favourite hobby, though, is drawing patterns. There's just one problem. Sometimes, Pansy forgets to draw the complete pattern. Maybe you can help. Try filling in the missing pieces in the patterns below.

1.

2.

3.

4.

5.

SUPER CHALLENGE: Draw a picture pattern of your own. Ask a classmate to fill in the missing pictures.

Tracing Leaves

Name ______________________________ Date ______________

Trace these leaf shapes onto tracing paper. Then, trace the outline from the tracing paper into the space on the right.

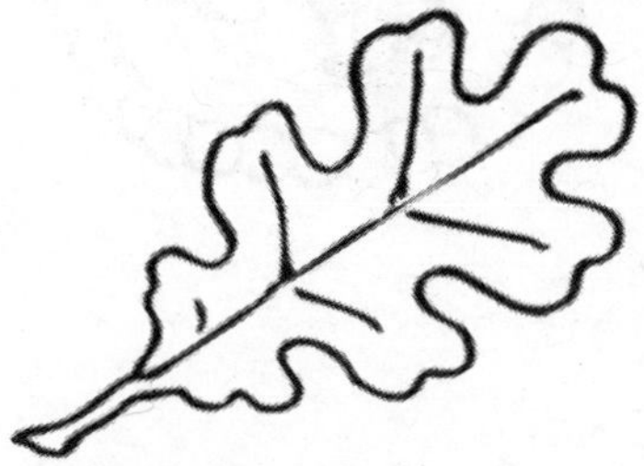

oak

clover

papaya

banana

money plant

Let's Design Jewellery

Name ______________________________ Date ______________

Design the following.

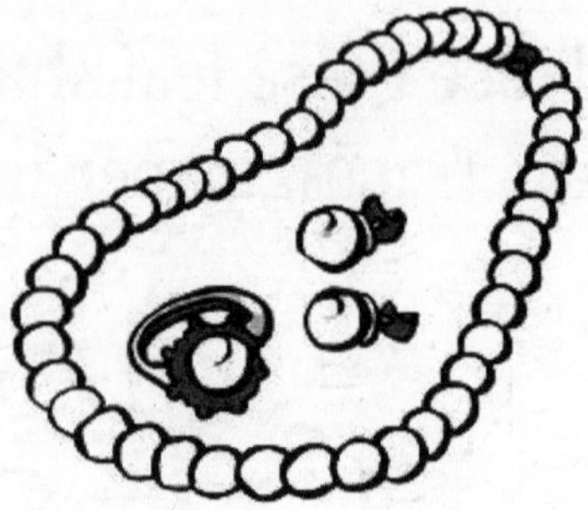

1. Earrings using shapes ▯ and ○.

2. Earrings using shapes ○ and △.

3. Necklace using the shape △.

4. Necklace using shapes ○ and ▭.

How Do I Look?

Name ______________________________ Date ______________

Draw glasses/spectacles on these faces using the given shapes:

Amount Counter

Name ______________________________ Date ____________

How many triangles and squares can you count in these geometric figures?

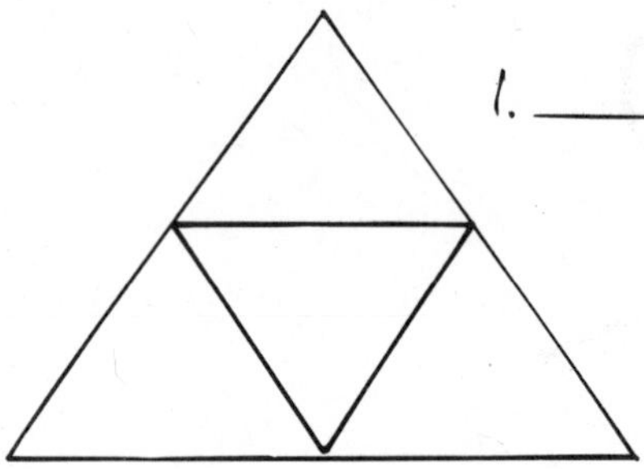

1. ______ TRIANGLES

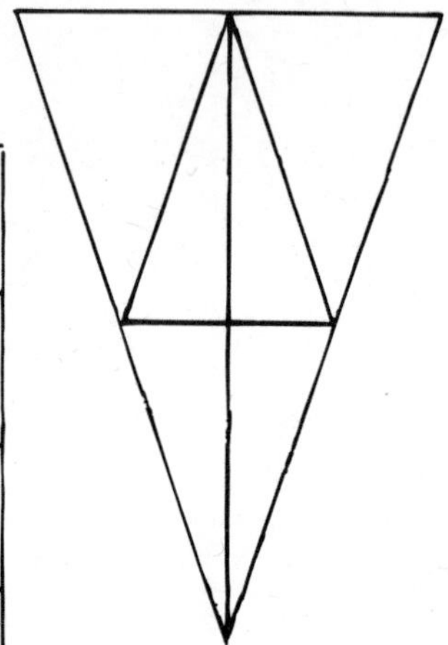

2. ______ TRIANGLES

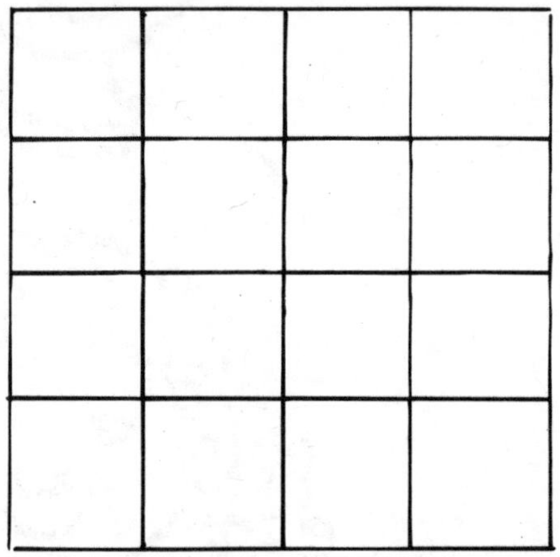

3. ______ SQUARES

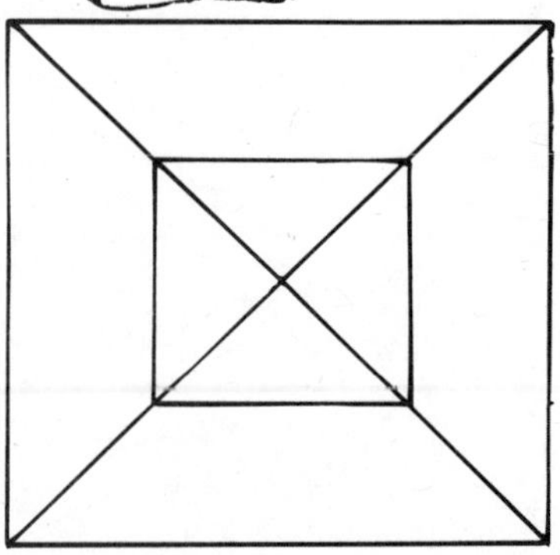

4. ______ TRIANGLES

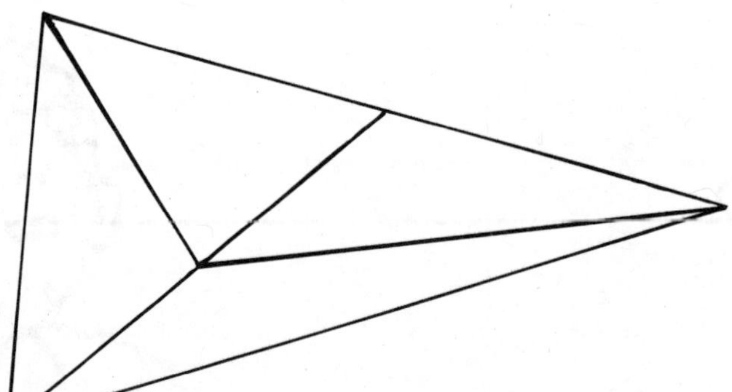

5. ______ TRIANGLES

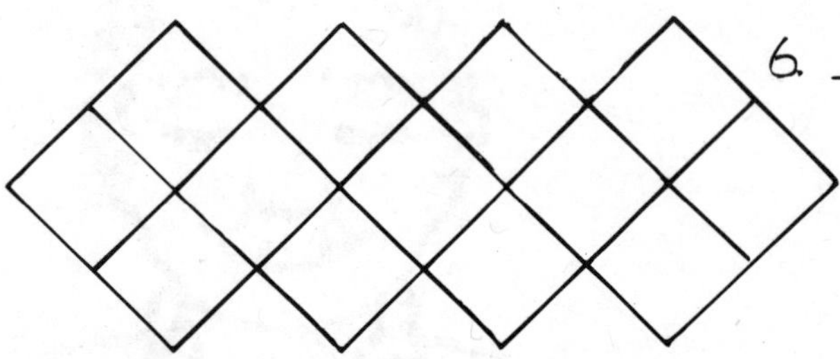

6. ______ SQUARES

How Much Can I Hold?

Name ____________________________________ Date ______________

Capacity is the maximum amount that something can contain.

Order these containers from <u>least</u> capacity (1) to <u>most</u> capacity (5).

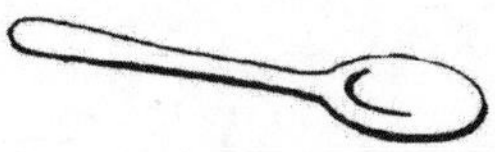

A. A table spoon

B. A cooking pot

C. A measuring cup

D. A bucket

E. A salt-shaker

We Carry Loads!

Name ______________________________ Date ______________

Look at these vehicles. They carry goods. They can only carry a certain amount according to their capacity.

Can you tell which vehicle carries which good? Match by drawing lines.

A. 

B. 

C. 

D. 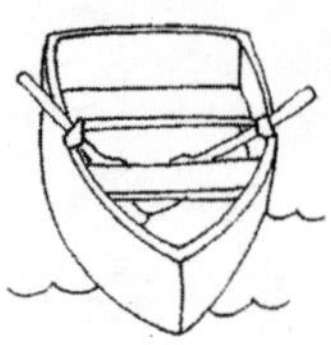

E. 

F. 

G. 

H. 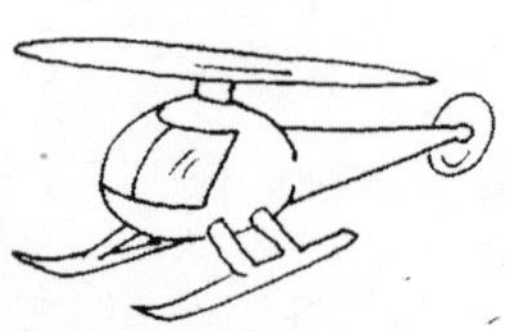

petrol/gas

helicopters

cement

water

houses

people

logs of wood

cartons/ boxes

rats

A Good Capacity

Name ______________________ Date __________

Here are some more things that have capacity, but not just for liquids and food. Match the pictures to the sentences at the bottom.

A. 

B. 

C. 

D. 

E. 

F. 

1. ____________ has a good capacity for chopped fruits.

2. ____________ has a good capacity to lift heavy weights.

3. ____________ has a good capacity to get angry.

4. ____________ has a good capacity to stock food.

5. ____________ has a good capacity to play for hours.

6. ____________ has a good capacity to read.

Ten at A Time

Name ______________________ Date ____________

Match the following:

1.	36	10 + 10 + 10 + 10 + 3	6 tens + 8 ones
2.	48	10 + 10 + 10 + 6	4 tens + 8 ones
3.	38	10 + 10 + 10 + 10 + 6	4 tens + 3 ones
4.	34	10 + 10 + 10 + 10 + 8	3 tens + 6 ones
5.	43	10 + 10 + 10 + 8	4 tens + 6 ones
6.	46	10 + 10 + 10 + 10 + 10 + 10 + 4	3 tens + 8 ones
7.	64	10 + 10 + 10 + 4	3 tens + 4 ones
8.	68	10 + 10 + 10 + 10 + 10 + 10 + 8	6 tens + 4 ones

Go Fish!

Name ______________________________ Date ______________

Govind is fishing for the right answers.
Can you help him. Connect the fish to the correct places blanks by drawing lines.

27 = ________ + 7

98 = ________ + 8

35 = ________ + 30

43 = ________ + 3

________ = 70 + 7

64 = ________ + 4

________ = 80 + 5

52 = 50 + ________

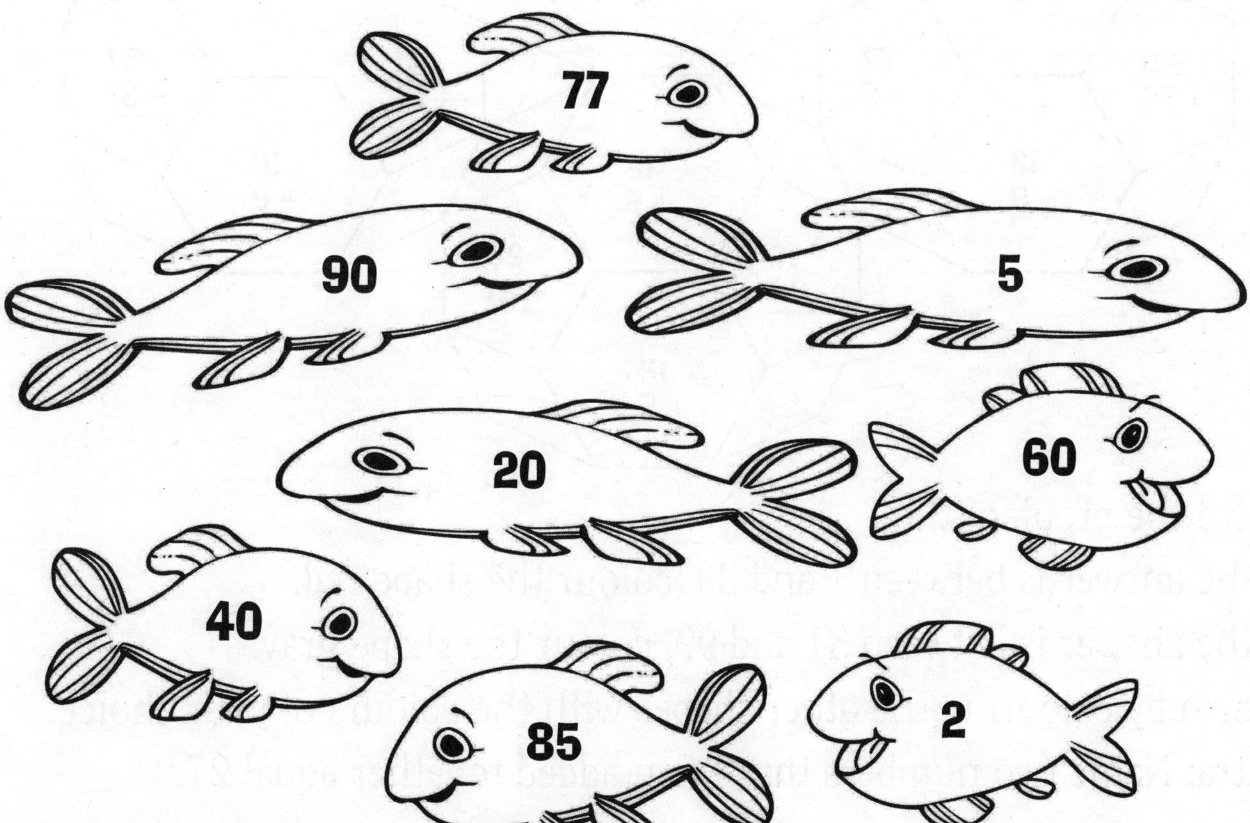

Kaleidoscope

Name ______________________ Date ____________

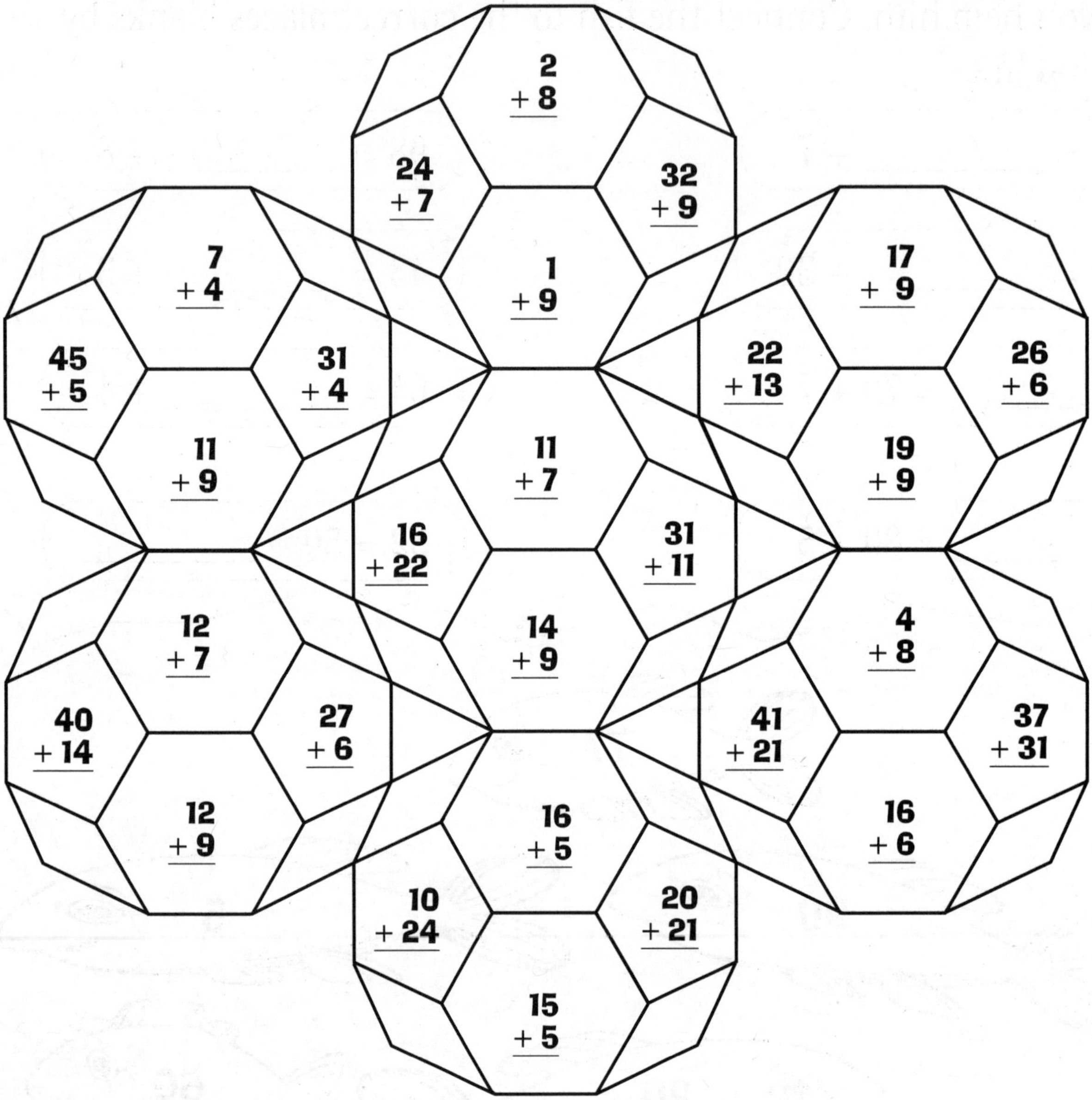

Solve the problems.

If the answer is between 1 and 30, colour the shape red.

If the answer is between 31 and 99, colour the shape gray.

Finish by colouring the other shapes with the colours of your choice.

Extra: Name two numbers that when added together equal 27.

Carnival Fun

Name ______________________________ Date ______________

Do the problems below. Then find your answers hidden in the carnival scene and circle them. Can you find all twelve answers?

15	27	34	15	16	12
33	23	23	25	14	31
+ 27	+ 12	+ 24	+ 10	+ 14	+ 17

28	43	10	29	37	51
22	27	17	13	31	23
+ 45	+ 27	+ 18	+ 16	+ 17	+ 17

How Many Days

Name ______________________________ Date ______________

Write the names of the months that have 31 days in the star and the ones that have 30 days in the moon. Which month got left out?

A Daily Puzzle

Name ____________________________ Date ______________

Rohan is puzzled. Can you help him fill in the blanks.

A. ____________________ comes after Tuesday.

B. ____________________ comes between Friday and Sunday.

C. ____________________ is two days before Saturday.

D. ____________________ comes before Wednesday.

E. ____________________ is the third day of the week.

F. ____________________ comes after Thursday.

G. ____________________ is the last day of the week.

Going Dotty

Name ______________________ Date ____________

Draw dots to complete the sentence

1.  + ☐ = 4

2. 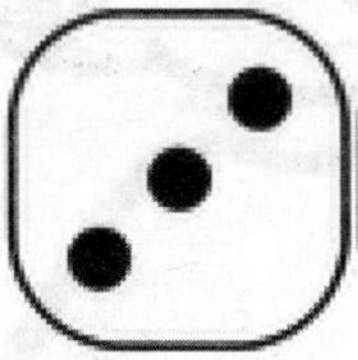 + ☐ = 8

3.  + ☐ = 9

4. 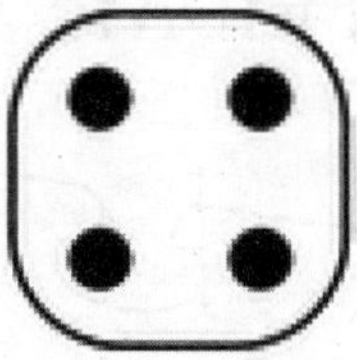 + ☐ = 8

5. 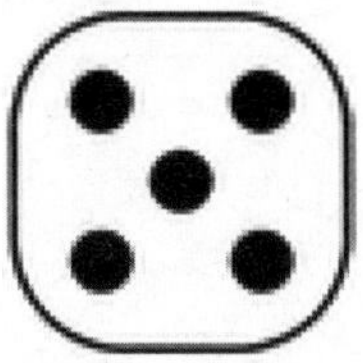 + ☐ = 10

6. ☐ + 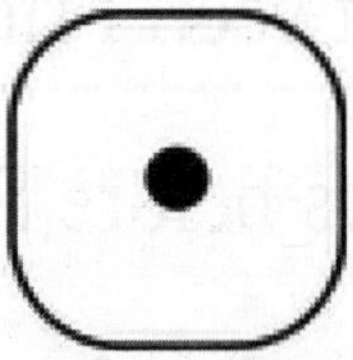 = 7

7. ☐ +  = 9

8. ☐ + 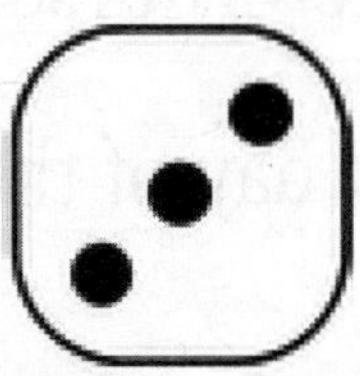 = 9

Totally Ten

Name ______________________________ Date ______________

A. 

How much more do you need to make 10? Draw the dots.

B. 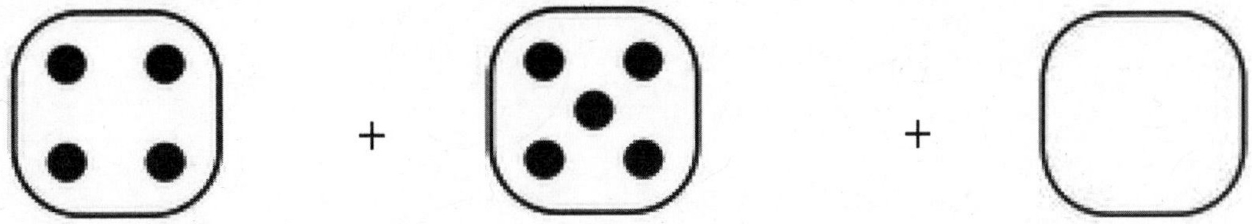

How much more do you need to make 10? Draw the dots.

C. 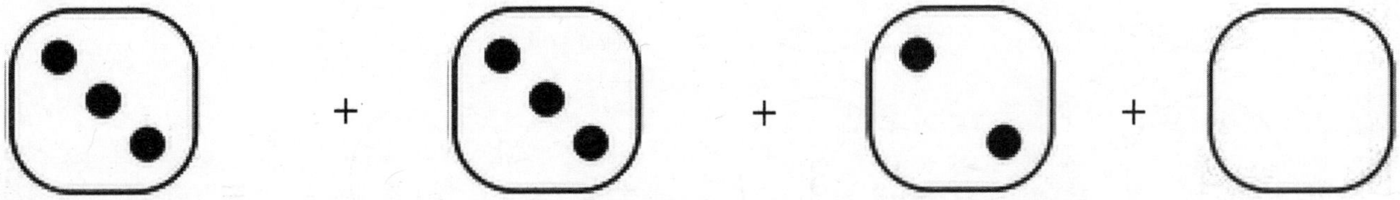

How much more do you need to make 10? Draw the dots.

D. 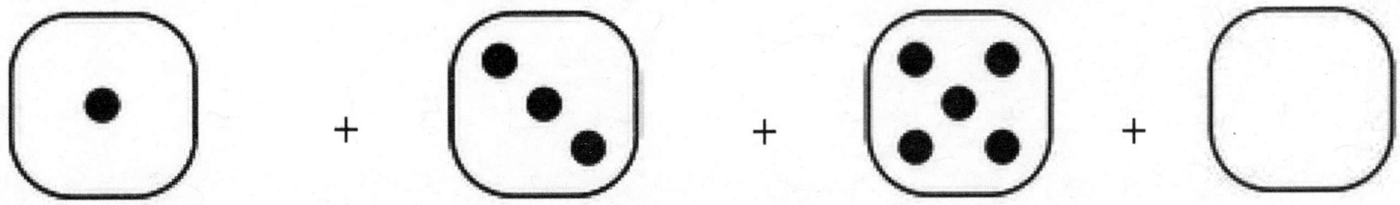

How much more do you need to make 10? Draw the dots.

E. 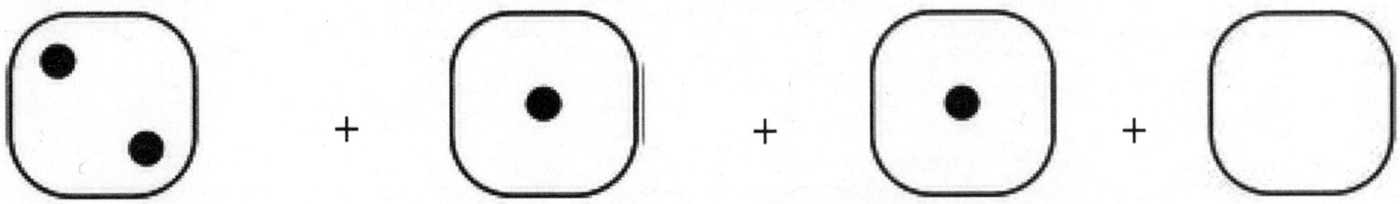

How much more do you need to make 10? Draw the dots.

F. 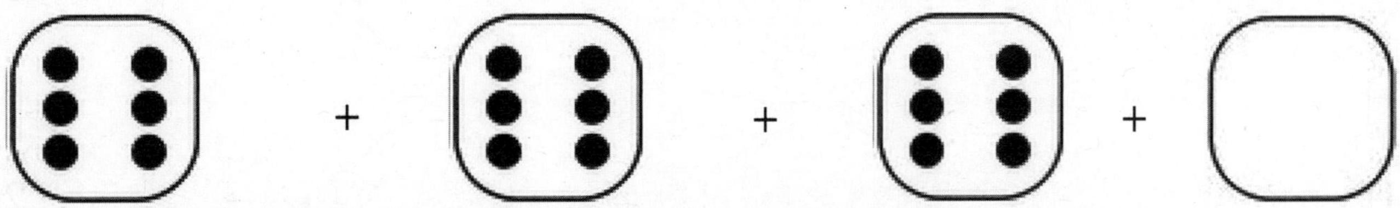

How much more do you need to make 20? Draw the dots.

Plenty Twenty

Name ______________________ Date ____________

Write different ways by which you can make 20, by writing a number in each empty circle.

A.	2	+	15	+		=	20
B.		+	16	+	1	=	20
C.	10	+		+	8	=	20
D.	4	+	3	+		=	20
E.	5	+		+	5	=	20
F.		+	1	+		=	20
G.		+		+		=	20
H.		+		+		=	20

Smart Adding

Name ______________________________ Date ______________

Sohan is adding three numbers at the same time. To make it easy, he first adds two numbers that 'make ten' and then adds the third number.

$$2 + \underbrace{3 + 7}_{10}$$

$$= 10 + 2$$

$$= 12$$

Can you use his trick and do these? Draw a line joining the two numbers you will add first.

1. 9 + 3 + 1 =

2. 6 + 8 + 4 =

3. 8 + 9 + 2 =

4. 7 + 3 + 8 =

5. 9 + 5 + 5 =

6. 6 + 9 + 1 =

7. 7 + 5 + 3 =

8. 7 + 6 + 4 =

Funny face

Name ______________________ Date ____________

Draw a joker face using:

- Curved lines for the: face, eyebrows, mouth
- Standing lines for the: nose, neck
- Standing lines for the: hair
- Sleeping lines for the: eyes

Do you want to add more lines to your drawing? Add them and write what type of lines you added.

Letters and Lines

Name ______________________________ Date ______________

Look at these letters. Count and write the number of standing lines, sleeping lines, slanting lines and curved lines each of them have.

C ______ Standing ______ Sleeping ______ Slanting ______ Curved

P ______ Standing ______ Sleeping ______ Slanting ______ Curved

A ______ Standing ______ Sleeping ______ Slanting ______ Curved

E ______ Standing ______ Sleeping ______ Slanting ______ Curved

J ______ Standing ______ Sleeping ______ Slanting ______ Curved

K ______ Standing ______ Sleeping ______ Slanting ______ Curved

Colour the Sunflower

Name ______________________ Date ____________

Do the addition problems in the sunflower picture below. Then use the Colour Key to tell you what colour to make each answer.
Extra: Write your age on four flashcards, and then add a 6, 7, 8, and 9 to each of the cards. Practise the answers with a friend.

Colour Key
56 = green
68 = orange
89 = yellow
97 = blue

Bewitching Math

Name ______________________________ Date ______________

Solve the problems. Then, connect the dot above each problem to the dot beside its answer. The first line has been drawn for you. Some dots will not be used.

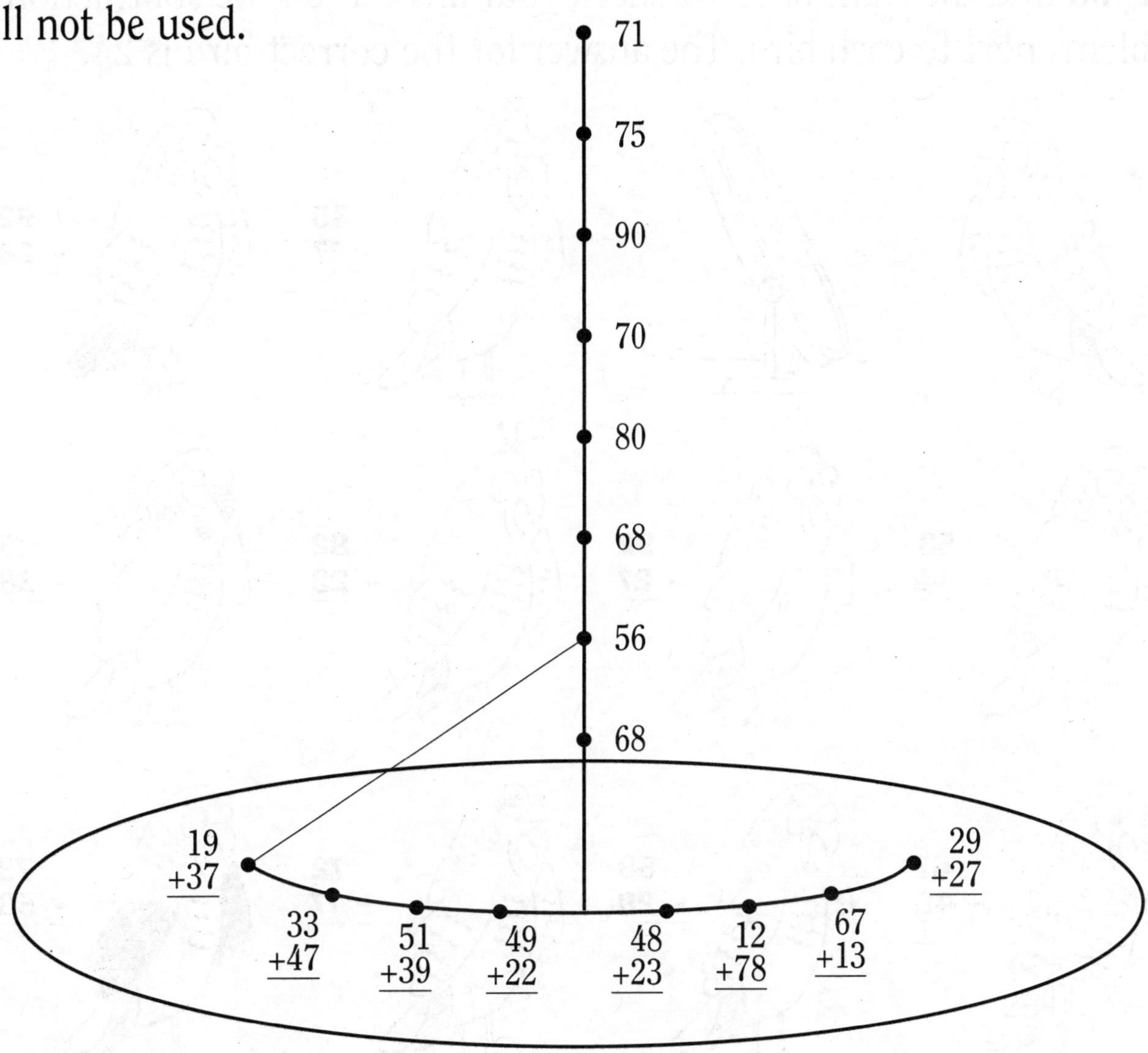

Taking It Further: Fill in the missing numbers in the problems below.

a.	b.	c.	d.	e.	f.
2☐	53	56	28	43	45
+27	+2☐	+1☐	+57	+☐7	+☐☐
50	82	73	☐☐	90	71

Purdy Bird

Name ______________________________ Date ______________

Purdy the Parakeet loves to look at herself in the mirror. Only one of these parakeets below really shows what Purdy looks like in the mirror. Can you find the right one? To check your answer, do the subtraction problems next to each bird. The answer for the correct bird is 24.

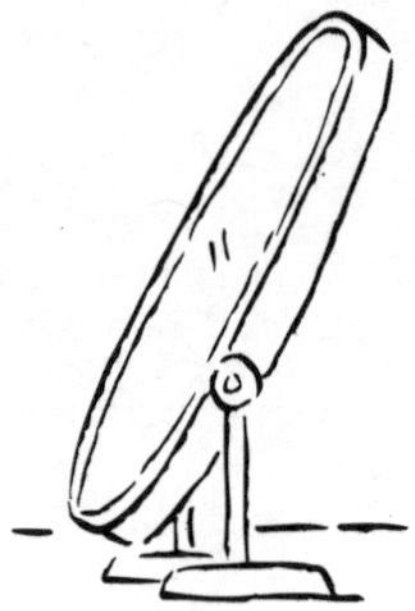

35
- 17

62
- 28

53
- 14

92
- 27

82
- 23

83
- 28

67
- 48

58
- 29

72
- 17

73
- 58

42
- 26

90
- 81

52
- 28

56
- 19

Stretching Taffy

Name ______________________________ Date ____________

Solve the problems. Then connect the dot below each problem on Line A to the dot beside its answer on Line C. The first line has been drawn for you. Connect the dot above each problem on Line B to the dot beside its answer on Line C. Some dots on Line C will not be used.

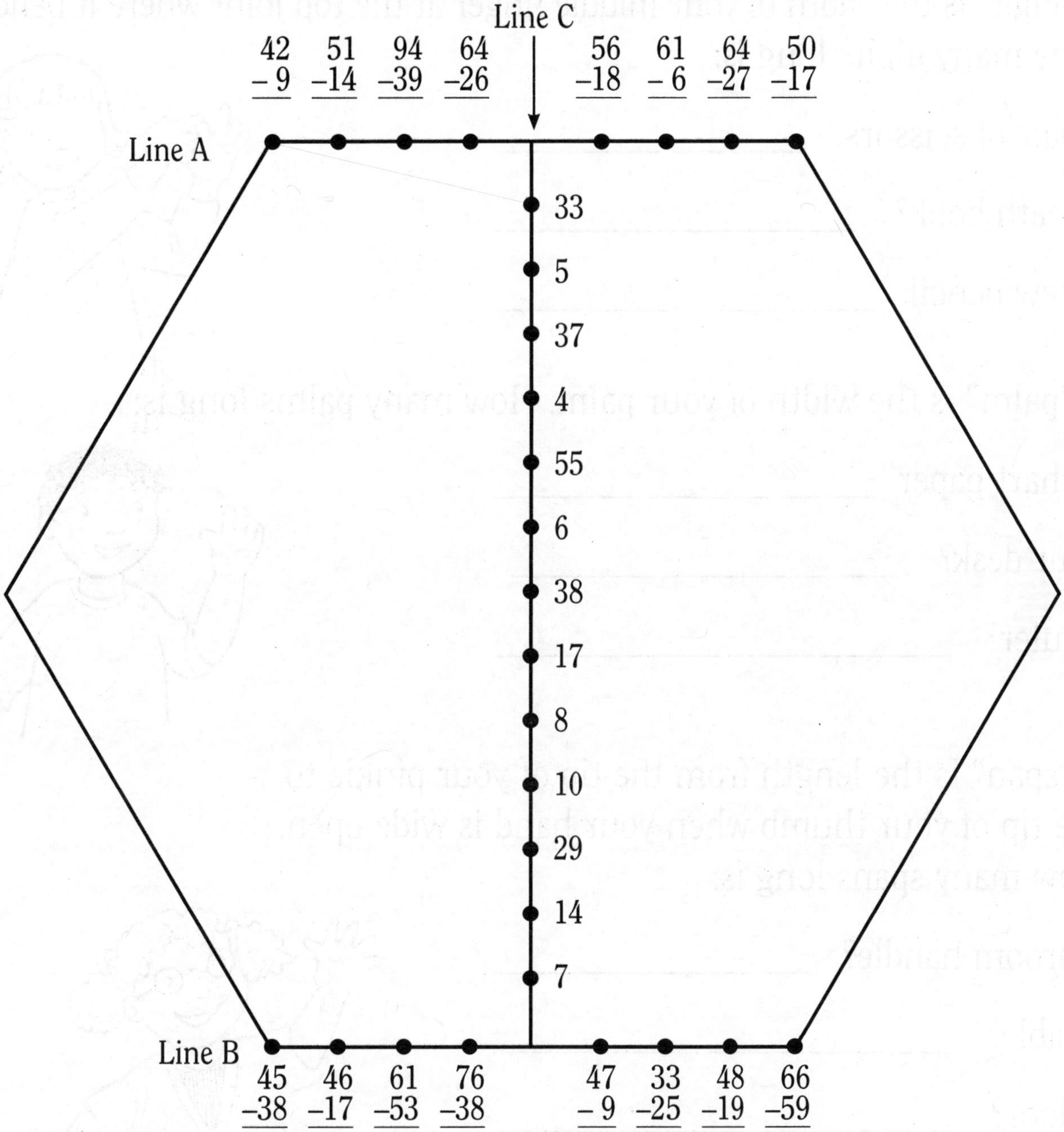

Taking It Further: Amanda picked 9 flowers from her garden and added them to some flowers in a vase. Now she has 16 flowers in all. How many flowers were in the vase to begin with? ________

Measuring Up

Name ______________________ Date ____________

People didn't always measure with rulers. Long ago, Egyptians and other people measured objects with body parts. Try it!

A "digit" is the width of your middle finger at the top joint where it bends. How many digits long is:

a pair of scissors? ______________

a math book? ______________

a new pencil ______________

A "palm" is the width of your palm. How many palms long is:

a chart paper ______________

your desk? ______________

a ruler? ______________

A "span" is the length from the tip of your pinkie to the tip of your thumb when your hand is wide open. How many spans long is:

a broom handle? ______________

a table? ______________

a door? ______________

"Finger-widths"

Name ______________________________ Date ______________

Things can be measured using finger-widths. Measure the objects below using finger-widths.

book

______ finger-widths

book

______ finger-widths

straw

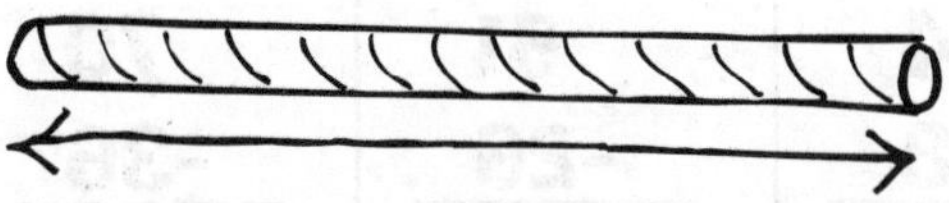

______ finger-widths

marker

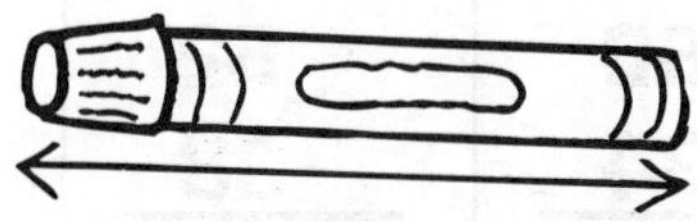

______ finger-widths

5 cubes

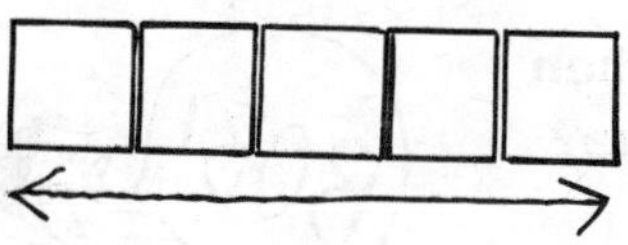

______ finger-widths

10 cubes

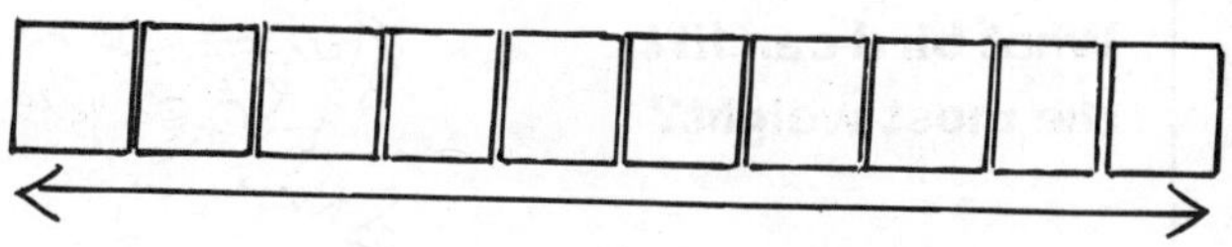

______ finger-widths

shoe

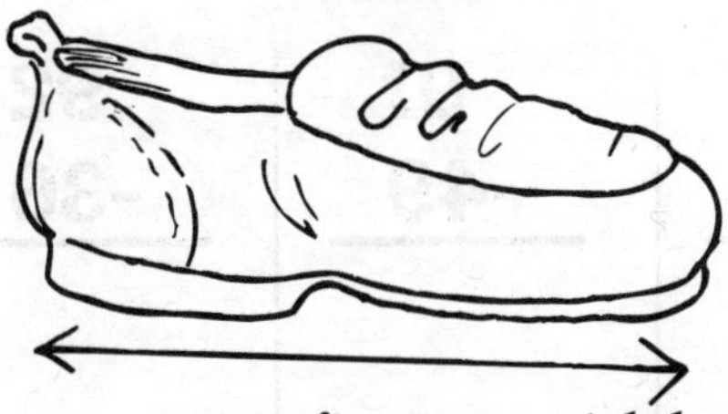

______ finger-widths

hand

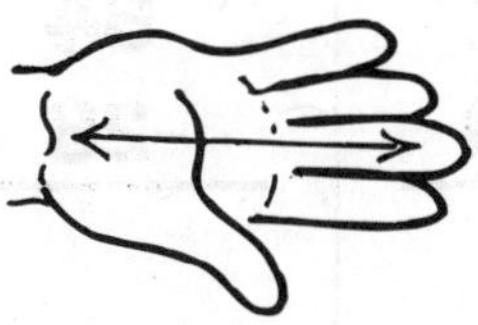

______ finger-widths

Riddle Subtraction

Name ______________________________ Date ______________

To find the answers to the riddles, solve the math problems. Write one number on each blank. The first one has been done for you. Then write the letters under each line in the boxes above that have the same number. When you have filled in all of the boxes with the right letters, you'll find out the answers to the riddles.

What has hands, but no feet and runs all day?

1.		2.	3.	4.	5.	6.

60 − 34	52 − 38	64 − 29
2 (C) 6 (K)	___ (A) ___ (O)	___ (L) ___ (C)

Where can you find cards on a ship?

1.	2.		3.	4.	5.	6.

44 − 28	51 − 26	70 − 36
___ (O) ___ (K)	___ (N) ___ (C)	___ (D) ___ (E)

What bird can lift the most weight?

1.		2.	3.	4.	5.	6.

41 − 29	64 − 28	81 − 36
___ (A) ___ (C)	___ (R) ___ (E)	___ (A) ___ (N)

What breaks when you say its name?

1.	2.	3.	4.	5.	6.	
						E

80 − 49	91 − 49	92 − 36
___ (L) ___ (S)	___ (E) ___ (I)	___ (N) ___ (C)

Bumping Billiard Balls

Name ______________________ Date __________

Match the following by drawing lines.

From......	Subtract......	And get......
87	27	31
58	33	54
94		60
		67
		61
		25

A Beautiful Sky

Name ______________________ Date ____________

If  is a ten and  is a one, then what happens in these situations. Draw your answer, then write your answer in numbers. The first one has been done for you.

1. There were 2 clouds and 1 bird. 2 clouds and 3 birds joined them.

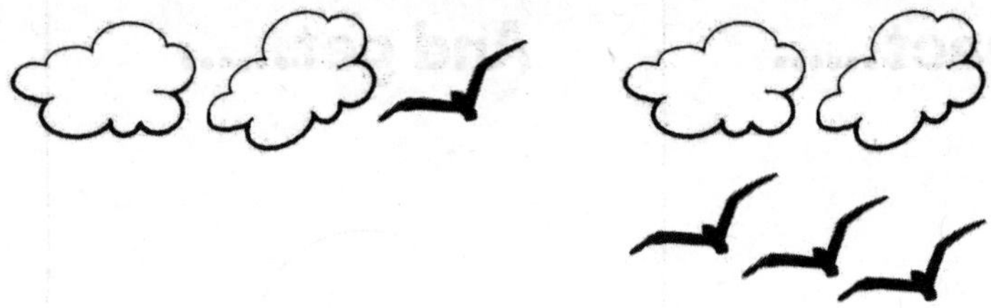

Ans: 5 clouds, 3 birds

= 50 + 3 = 53

2. There were 5 clouds and 2 birds. 1 cloud rolled away and 1 bird flew off.

Ans: ______________

= ______________

3. There were 4 clouds and 7 birds. 1 more cloud came along and 5 birds flew away.

Ans: ______________

= ______________

Reading Books

Name ______________________________ Date ______________

This table shows how many books Diya, Adit, Dheer and Pia read last month.

Diya	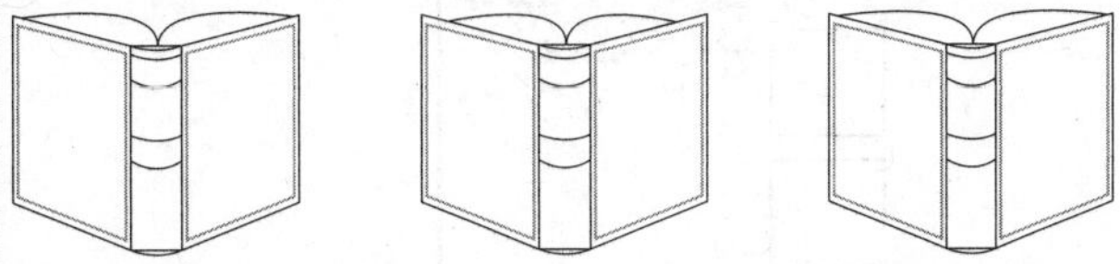
Adit	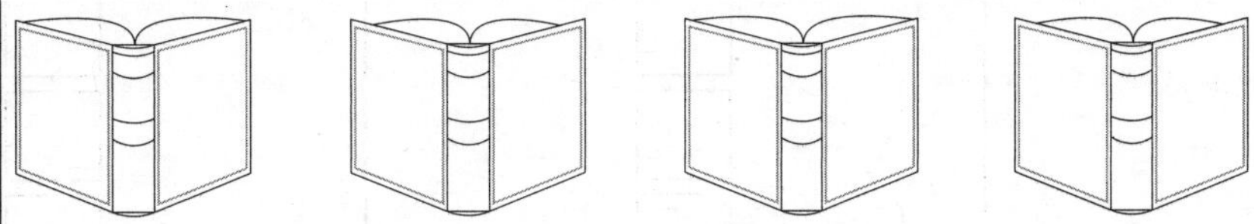
Dheer	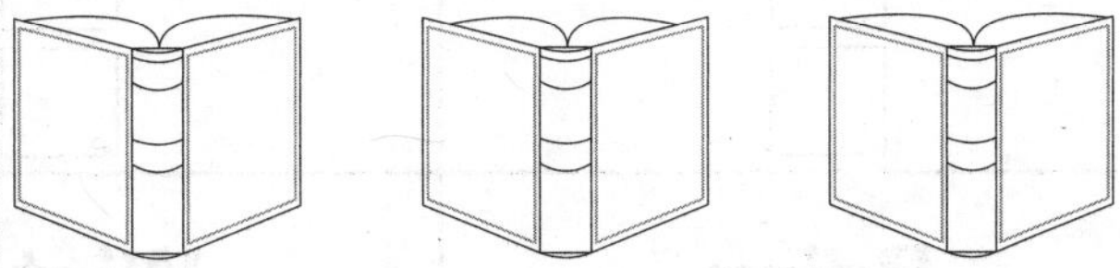
Pia	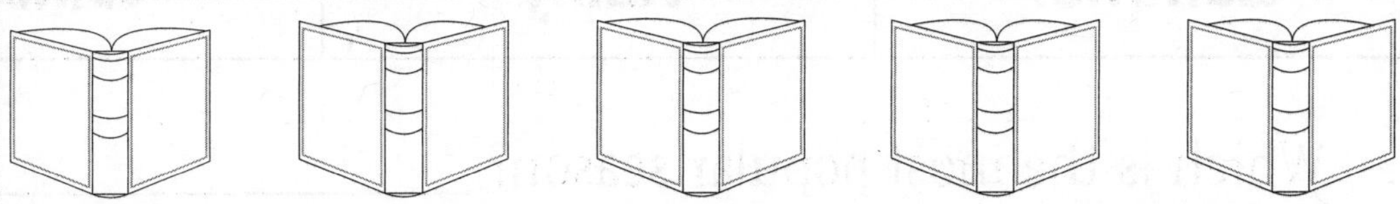

1. Who read the most books? ____________
2. Which two children read the same number of books? ____________
3. Who read one book more then Dheer? ____________
4. How many more books should Dheer have read to catch up to Pia? __
5. What is the total number of books read by all four children? ________

My Favourite Season

Name ______________________________ Date ____________

This table shows 15 people's favourite season.

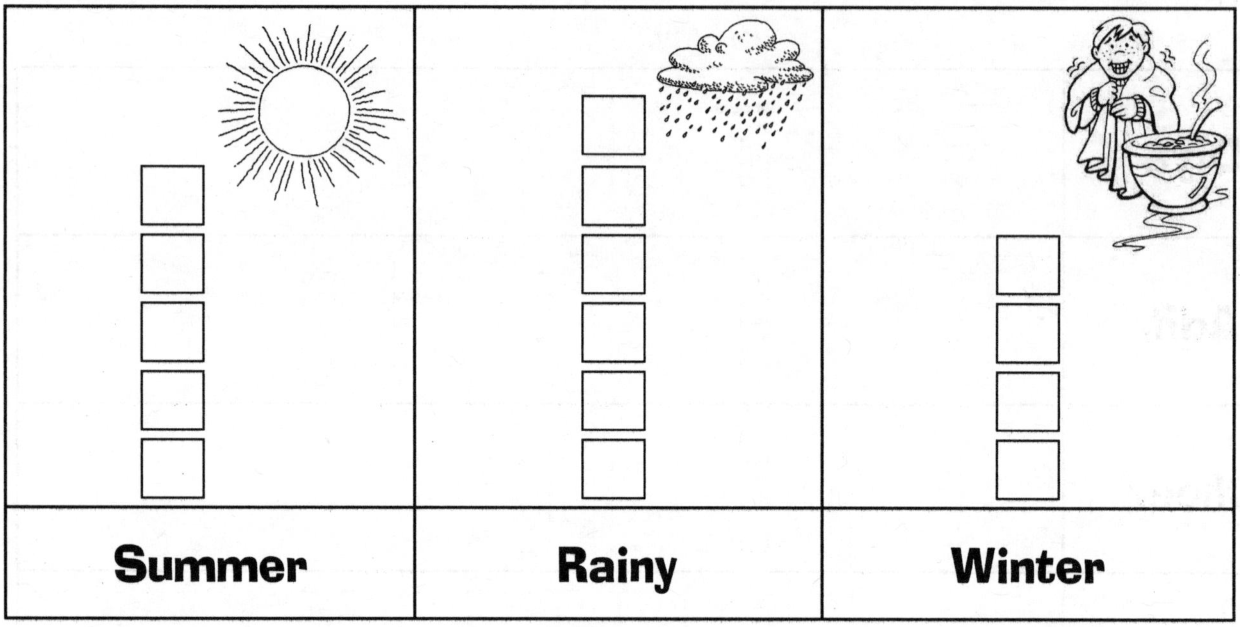

1. Which is the most popular season? ____________________

2. Which is the least popular season? ____________________

3. How many people like summer? ____________________

4. If ____________________ got one more vote, it would be as popular as____________________.

5. How many people do not like winter? ____________________

Answer Key

Page 5

1. square, 4, 4;
2. triangle 3, 3;
3. circle, 0, 0;
4. petagon, 5, 5;
5-6. Answers will vary.

Page 6

A. 1F, 2G, 3B, 4C **or** A, 5E, 6I, 7E, 8H, 9G, 10G, 11C
B. 1B, 2F, 3C, 4I, 5F, 6E, 7A, 8D, 9I, 10F, 11I
C. 1H, 2C, 3C, 4G, 5G, 6C, 7F, 8I, 9B, 10C **or** A, 11F

Page 7

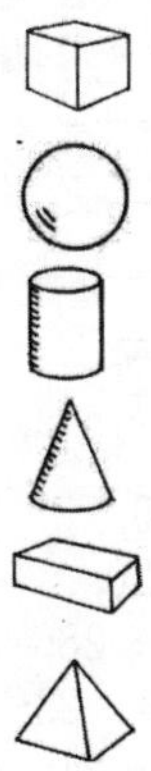

Roll	Slide	Spin
	✓	
✓		✓
✓	✓	
✓	✓	✓
	✓	
	✓	✓

Page 8

Answers will vary. Make sure that students have oriented the blocks correctly in order to maximise height; also that the stacking is appropriate.

Page 9

1. 167; **2.** 34, 35; **3.** 42, 43; **4.** 16, 18
5. 73, 74, 75; **6.** 31, 32; **7.** 10 12 14 16
8. 15 18 21 24; **9.** 83, 84, 85, 86, 87, 88
10. after; **11.** before; **12.** after
13. before; **14.** before; **15.** before

Page 10

1. 5+ 5;
2. 6 + 4;
3. 6 + 6;
4. 2 + 3 + 4;
5. 3 + 3 + 3

Page 11

1. 2, 4, 6, 8;
2. 4, 8, 12, 16;
3. 6, 12, 18, 24;
4. 8, 16, 24, 32;
5. 10, 20, 30, 40, 50, 60, 70, 80, 90, 100

Page 12

1. 3, 2;
2. 2, 4;
3. 2, 5;
4. 4, 3

Page 13

Seal, Deer, Lion, Beer.
Drawings will vary. Make sure the size of the animal relative to the seal and the deer is appropriate.

Page 14

1. B; **2.** B; **3.** B; **4.** C

Pages 15

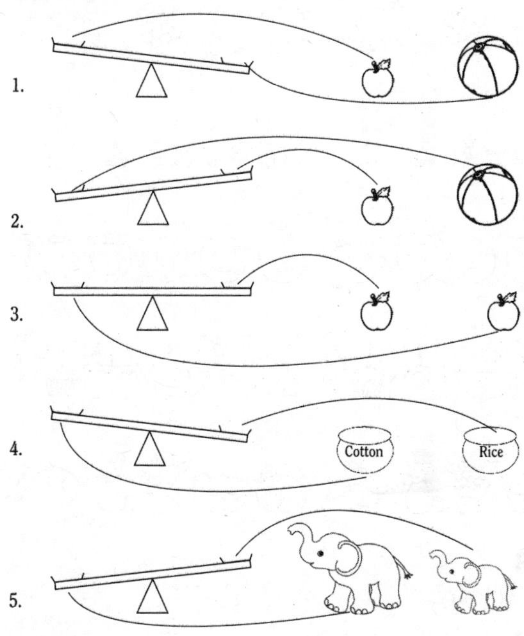

Page 16

Rishabh: 22;
Lalit: 14;
Mansi: 33;
Sarah: 41;
Mini: 37

Page 17

1. 23; **2.** 31; **3.** 14; **4.** 27; **5.** 42

Page 18

1. 32, 42, 52, 62, 72, 82, 92;
2. 70, 60, 50, 40, 30, 20, 10;
3. 67, 57, 47, 37, 27, 17, 7;
4. 44, 55, 66, 77, 88, 99

Page 19
1. Answers will vary.
2. Numbers will be coloured in using an AB pattern of red and blue.

Page 20
A: 23 should be 20;
B: 7 should be 8;
C: 4 should be 13;
D: 24 should be 28

Page 21
A: 7, 11, 15;
B: 5, 8, 11;
C: 10, 18, 26;
D: 20, 25, 30;
E: 15, 22, 29;
F: 9, 18, 27

Page 22

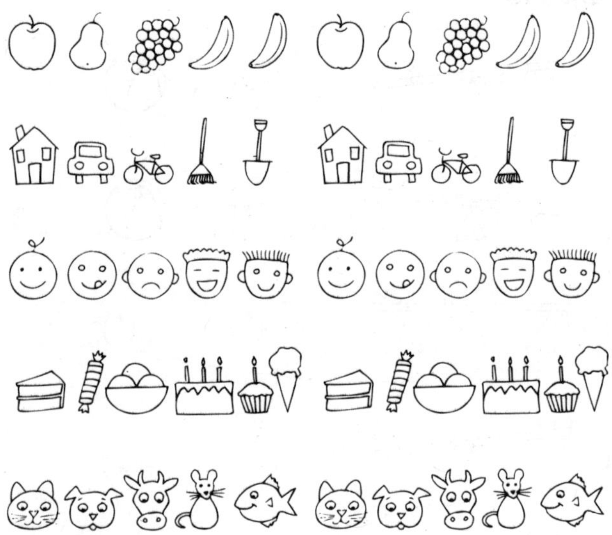

Page 23
Drawings will vary.

Page 24
Drawings will vary.

Page 25
Drawings will vary.

Page 26
1. 5; **2.** 11; **3.** 30; **4.** 12; **5.** 8; **6.** 17

Page 27
A. 1; **B.** 4; **C.** 3; **D.** 5; **E.** 2

Page 28
A. cartons/boxes;
B. people;
C. logs of wood;
D. people;
E. cement;
F. petroleum/gas;
G. water;
H. people

Page 29
1. D; **2.** B; **3.** E; **4.** A; **5.** F; **6.** C

Page 30
1. 36 = 10 + 10 + 10 + 6 = 3 tens + 6 ones
2. 48 = 10 + 10 + 10 + 10 + 8 = 4 tens + 8 ones
3. 38 = 10 + 10 + 10 + 8 = 3 tens + 8 ones
4. 34 = 10 + 10 + 10 + 4 = 3 tens + 4 ones
5. 43 = 10 + 10 + 10 + 10 + 3 = 4 tens + 3 ones
6. 46 = 10 + 10 + 10 + 10 +6 = 4 tens + 6 ones
7. 64 = 10 + 10 + 10 + 10 + 10 +10 + 4 = 6 tens + 4 ones
8. 68 = 10 + 10 + 10 + 10 + 10 +10 + 8 = 6 tens + 8 ones

Page 31

27 = 20 + 7	98 = 90 + 8
35 = 5 + 30	43 = 40 + 3
77 = 70 + 7	64 = 60 + 4
85 = 80 + 5	52 = 50 + 2

Page 32
2 + 8 = 10; 24 + 7 = 31; 32 + 9 = 41; 1 + 9 = 10;
7 + 4 = 11; 45 + 5 = 50; 31 + 4 = 35; 11 + 9 = 20;
17 + 9 = 26; 22 + 13 = 35; 26 + 6 = 32; 19 + 9 = 28;
11 + 7 = 18; 16 + 22 = 38; 31 + 11 = 42; 14 + 9 = 23;
12 + 7 = 19; 40 + 14 = 54; 27 + 6 = 33; 12 + 9 = 21;
4 + 8 = 12; 41 + 21 = 62; 37 + 31 = 68; 16 + 6 = 22;
16 + 5 = 21; 10 + 24 = 34; 20 + 21 = 41; 15 + 5 = 20
Extra: Answers will vary.

Page 33
15 + 33 + 27 = 75; 27 + 23 + 12 = 62;
34 + 23 + 24 = 81; 15 + 25 + 10 = 50;
16 + 14 + 14 = 44; 12 + 31 + 17 = 60;
28 + 22 + 45 = 95; 43 + 27 + 27 = 97;
10 + 17 + 18 = 45; 29 + 13 + 16 = 58;
37 + 31 + 17 = 85; 51 + 23 + 17 = 91

Page 34
Months in the star: January, March, May, July, August, October, December
Months in the moon: April, June, September, November
Months left out: February

Page 35
A. Wednesday;
B. Saturday;
C. Thursday;
D. Tuesday;
E Wednesday (assuming Monday as the first day of the week);
F. Friday;
G. Sunday

Page 36

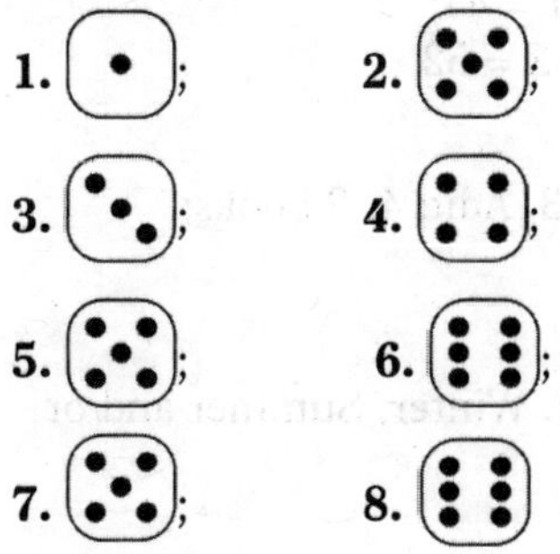

Page 37

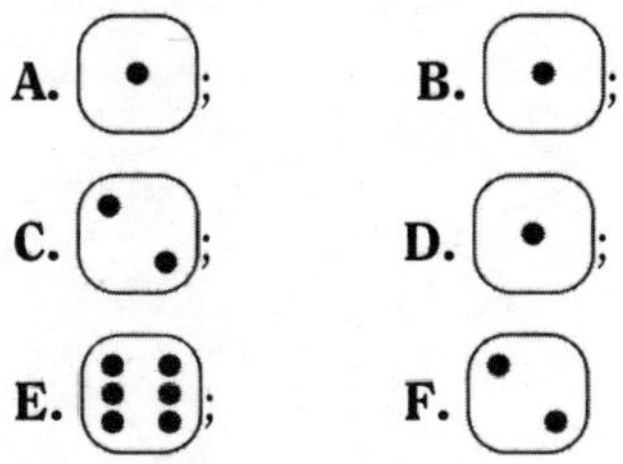

Page 38

A. 3; **B.** 3; **C.** 2; **D.** 13;
E. 10; **F**-H; Answers will vary.

Page 39

1. 9 + 3 + 1 = 10 + 3 = 13
2. 6 + 8 + 4 = 10 + 8 = 18
3. 8 + 9 + 2 = 10 + 9 = 19
4. 7 + 3 + 8 = 10 + 8 = 18
5. 9 + 5 + 5 = 10 + 9 =19
6. 6 + 9 + 1 = 10 + 6 = 16
7. 7 + 5 + 3 = 10 + 5 = 15
8. 7 + 6 + 4 = 10 + 7 = 17

Page 40

Drawing will vary. Make students have used the correct lines at the correct places.

Page 41

C has 1 curved line; P has 1 standing and 1 curved line; A has 2 slanting and 1 sleeping lines; E has 1 standing and 3 sleeping lines; J has 1 standing and 1 curved line, K has 1 standing and 2 slanting lines.

Page 42

32 + 24 = 56; 16 + 40 = 56; 54 + 14 = 68
77 + 12 = 89; 34 + 34 = 68; 53 + 36 = 89
26 + 63 = 89; 23 + 45 = 68; 35 + 62 = 97
38 + 30 = 68; 22 + 67 = 89; 47 + 42 = 89
51 + 17 = 68; 71 + 18 = 89; 46 + 22 = 68
33 + 23 = 56; 44 + 12 = 56

Page 43

19 + 37 = 56; 33 + 47 = 80; 51 + 39 = 90;
49 + 22 = 71; 48 + 23 = 71; 12 + 78 = 90;
67 + 13 = 80; 29 + 27 = 56

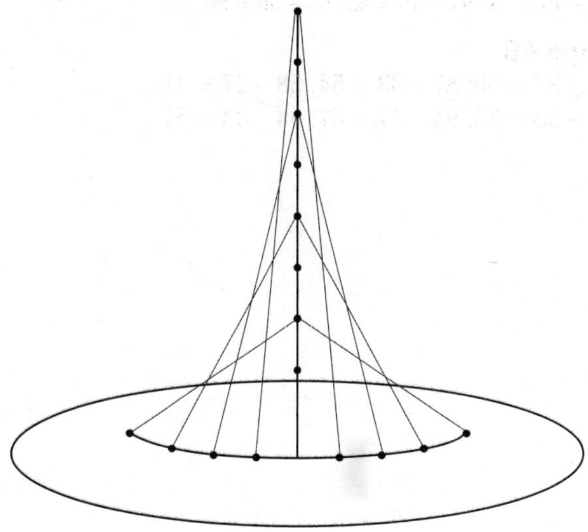

a. 3 **b.** 9 **c.** 7 **d.** 85 **e.** 4 **f.** 26

Page 44

35 – 17 = 18; 62 – 28 = 34; 53 – 14 = 39; 92 – 27 = 65
82 – 23 = 59; 83 – 28 = 55; 67 – 48 = 19; 58 – 29 = 29
72 – 17 = 55; 73 – 58 = 15; 42 – 26 = 16; 90 – 81 = 9
52 – 28 = 24; 56 – 19 = 37

Page 45

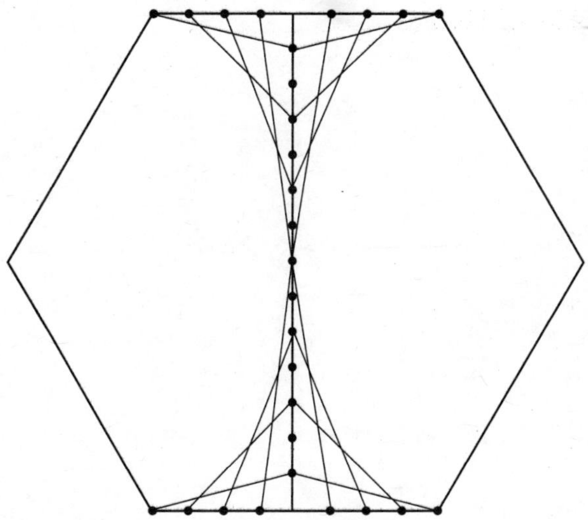

7 flowers

Page 46

Answers will vary.

Page 47

Answers will vary.

Page 48

A CLOCK
60 – 34 = 26; 52 – 38 = 14; 64 – 29 = 35
ON DECK
44 – 28 = 16; 51 – 26 = 25; 70 – 36 = 34
A CRANE
41 – 29 = 12; 64 – 28 = 36; 81 – 36 = 45
SILENCE
80 – 49 = 31; 91 – 49 = 42; 92 – 36 = 56

Page 49

87 – 27 = 60; 87 – 33 = 54; 58 – 27 = 31; 58 – 33 = 25; 94 – 27 = 67; 94 – 33 = 61

Page 50

2. 4 clouds, 1 bird = 40 + 1 = 41;
3. 5 clouds, 2 birds = 50 + 2 = 52

Page 51

1. Pia; **2.** Diya and Dheer; **3.** Adit; **4.** 2 books; **5.** 15 books

Page 52

1. Rainy; **2.** Winter; **3.** 5; **4.** Winter, Summer and/or Summer, Rainy; **5.** 11